This Gardening Journal Belongs To:

_____

Gardening PROJECTS

YEARLY GOALS

NEW PROJECTS

TECHNIQUES

NOTES

Gardening PROJECTS

YEARLY GOALS

NEW PROJECTS

TECHNIQUES

NOTES

Seasonal To Do List

SPRING

SUMMER

FALL

WINTER

Notes

Seasonal To Do List

SPRING

- [ ]
- [ ]
- [ ]
- [ ]
- [ ]
- [ ]
- [ ]
- [ ]

SUMMER

- [ ]
- [ ]
- [ ]
- [ ]
- [ ]
- [ ]
- [ ]
- [ ]

FALL

- [ ]
- [ ]
- [ ]
- [ ]
- [ ]
- [ ]
- [ ]
- [ ]

WINTER

- [ ]
- [ ]
- [ ]
- [ ]
- [ ]
- [ ]
- [ ]
- [ ]

Notes

Gardening Expenses

ITEM#	DESCRIPTION	QTY	PRICE	NOTES

TOTAL EXPENSES

Gardening Expenses

ITEM#	DESCRIPTION	QTY	PRICE	NOTES

TOTAL EXPENSES

Gardening Expenses

ITEM#	DESCRIPTION	QTY	PRICE	NOTES

TOTAL EXPENSES

Gardening Expenses

ITEM#	DESCRIPTION	QTY	PRICE	NOTES

TOTAL EXPENSES

Plant Name   **Date Planted**

Water Requirements   💧   💧💧   💧💧💧   Sunlight ☀ ☼ ●

☐ Seed   ☐ Transplant

Date	Event

Notes

Outcome

Uses

Purchased at: _____   Price: _____

Gardening Notes

Plant Name	**Date Planted**

Water Requirements 💧 💧💧 💧💧💧   Sunlight ☀ ☼ ●

☐ Seed   ☐ Transplant

Date	Event

Notes

Outcome

Uses

Purchased at: _____   Price: _____

Gardening Notes

Plant Name | **Date Planted**

Water Requirements   💧 💧💧 💧💧💧

Sunlight   ☀ ◐ ●

☐ Seed   ☐ Transplant

Date	Event

Notes

Outcome

Uses

Purchased at: _____   Price: _____

Gardening Notes

Plant Name | **Date Planted**

Water Requirements 💧 💧💧 💧💧💧

Sunlight ☀ ☼ ●

☐ Seed   ☐ Transplant

Date	Event

Notes

Outcome

Uses

Purchased at: _____   Price: _____

Gardening Notes

Plant Name **Date Planted**

Water Requirements 💧 💧💧 💧💧💧

Sunlight ☀️ 🌤 ●

☐ Seed   ☐ Transplant

Date	Event

Notes

Outcome

Uses

Purchased at: _____ Price: _____

Gardening Notes

Plant Name | **Date Planted**

Water Requirements 💧 💧💧 💧💧💧 | Sunlight ☀ ☼ ●

☐ Seed ☐ Transplant

Date	Event

Notes

Outcome

Uses

Purchased at: _____ Price: _____

Gardening Notes

Plant Name	Date Planted

Water Requirements 💧 💧💧 💧💧💧

Sunlight ☀ ☀/☽ ●

☐ Seed ☐ Transplant

Date	Event

Notes

Outcome

Uses

Purchased at: _____ Price: _____

Gardening Notes

Plant Name **Date Planted**

Water Requirements 💧 💧💧 💧💧💧   Sunlight ☀ ☼ ●

☐ Seed   ☐ Transplant

Date	Event

Notes

Outcome

Uses

Purchased at: _____   Price: _____

Gardening Notes

Plant Name | **Date Planted**

Water Requirements 💧 💧💧 💧💧💧   Sunlight ☀ ☼ ●

☐ Seed   ☐ Transplant

Date	Event

Notes

Outcome

Uses

Purchased at: _____   Price: _____

Gardening Notes

Plant Name | **Date Planted**

Water Requirements 💧 💧💧 💧💧💧

Sunlight ☀ ☼ ●

☐ Seed   ☐ Transplant

Date	Event

Notes

Outcome

Uses

Purchased at: _____   Price: _____

Gardening Notes

Plant Name | **Date Planted**

Water Requirements 💧 💧💧 💧💧💧   Sunlight ☀ ☼ ●

☐ Seed   ☐ Transplant

Date	Event

Notes

Outcome

Uses

Purchased at: _____   Price: _____

Gardening Notes

Plant Name | **Date Planted**

Water Requirements 💧 💧💧 💧💧💧

Sunlight ☀ ☼ ●

☐ Seed   ☐ Transplant

Date	Event

Notes

Outcome

Uses

Purchased at: _____   Price: _____

Gardening Notes

Plant Name   **Date Planted**

Water Requirements   💧   💧💧   💧💧💧   Sunlight ☀ ☼ ●

☐ Seed   ☐ Transplant

Date	Event

Notes

Outcome

Uses

Purchased at: _____   Price: _____

Gardening Notes

Plant Name | **Date Planted**

Water Requirements 💧 💧💧 💧💧💧

Sunlight ☀ ☼ ●

☐ Seed   ☐ Transplant

Date	Event

Notes

Outcome

Uses

Purchased at: _____   Price: _____

Gardening Notes

Plant Name | **Date Planted**

Water Requirements 💧 💧💧 💧💧💧   Sunlight ☀ ☼ ●

☐ Seed   ☐ Transplant

Date	Event

Notes

Outcome

Uses

Purchased at: _____   Price: _____

Gardening Notes

Plant Name	Date Planted

Water Requirements 💧 💧💧 💧💧💧

Sunlight ☀ ☼ ●

☐ Seed   ☐ Transplant

Date	Event

Notes

Outcome

Uses

Purchased at: _____   Price: _____

Gardening Notes

Plant Name | **Date Planted**

Water Requirements 💧 💧💧 💧💧💧

Sunlight ☀ ☼ ●

☐ Seed   ☐ Transplant

Date	Event

Notes

Outcome

Uses

Purchased at: _____   Price: _____

Gardening Notes

Plant Name **Date Planted**

Water Requirements 💧 💧💧 💧💧💧   Sunlight ☀ ☼ ●

☐ Seed   ☐ Transplant

Date	Event

Notes

Outcome

Uses

Purchased at: _____   Price: _____

Gardening Notes

Plant Name | **Date Planted**

Water Requirements 💧 💧💧 💧💧💧   Sunlight ☀ ☼ ●

☐ Seed   ☐ Transplant

Date	Event

Notes

Outcome

Uses

Purchased at: _____   Price: _____

Gardening Notes

| **Plant Name** | **Date Planted** |

Water Requirements 💧 💧💧 💧💧💧   Sunlight ☀ 🌤 ●

☐ Seed   ☐ Transplant

Date	Event

Notes

Outcome

Uses

Purchased at: _____   Price: _____

Gardening Notes

Plant Name	**Date Planted**

Water Requirements 💧 💧💧 💧💧💧   Sunlight ☀ ☼ ●

☐ Seed   ☐ Transplant

Date	Event

Notes

Outcome

Uses

Purchased at: _____   Price: _____

Gardening Notes

Plant Name | **Date Planted**

Water Requirements 💧 💧💧 💧💧💧

Sunlight ☀ ☼ ●

☐ Seed   ☐ Transplant

Date	Event

Notes

Outcome

Uses

Purchased at: _____   Price: _____

Gardening Notes

Plant Name   **Date Planted**

Water Requirements   💧   💧💧   💧💧💧   Sunlight ☀ ☼ ●

☐ Seed   ☐ Transplant

Date	Event

Notes

Outcome

Uses

Purchased at: _____   Price: _____

Gardening Notes

Plant Name | **Date Planted**

Water Requirements 💧 💧💧 💧💧💧 | Sunlight ☀ ☼ ●

☐ Seed ☐ Transplant

Date	Event

Notes

Outcome

Uses

Purchased at: _____ Price: _____

Gardening Notes

Plant Name	Date Planted

Water Requirements 💧 💧💧 💧💧💧

Sunlight ☀ ☼ ●

☐ Seed ☐ Transplant

Date	Event

Notes

Outcome

Uses

Purchased at: _____ Price: _____

Gardening Notes

Plant Name | **Date Planted**

Water Requirements 💧 💧💧 💧💧💧   Sunlight ☀ ☼ ●

☐ Seed ☐ Transplant

Date	Event

Notes

Outcome

Uses

Purchased at: _____ Price: _____

Gardening Notes

Plant Name **Date Planted**

Water Requirements 💧 💧💧 💧💧💧   Sunlight ☀ ☼ ●

☐ Seed   ☐ Transplant

Date	Event

Notes

Outcome

Uses

Purchased at: _____   Price: _____

Gardening Notes

| **Plant Name** | **Date Planted** |

Water Requirements 💧 💧💧 💧💧💧   Sunlight ☀ ☼ ●

☐ Seed   ☐ Transplant

Date	Event

Notes

Outcome

Uses

Purchased at: _____   Price: _____

Gardening Notes

Plant Name | **Date Planted**

Water Requirements 💧 💧💧 💧💧💧   Sunlight ☀ 🌤 ●

☐ Seed   ☐ Transplant

Date	Event

Notes

Outcome

Uses

Purchased at: _____   Price: _____

Gardening Notes

Plant Name | **Date Planted**

Water Requirements 💧 💧💧 💧💧💧

Sunlight ☀ ☼ ●

☐ Seed   ☐ Transplant

Date	Event

Notes

Outcome

Uses

Purchased at: _____   Price: _____

Gardening Notes

Plant Name | **Date Planted**

Water Requirements 💧 💧💧 💧💧💧   Sunlight ☀ ☀ ●

☐ Seed   ☐ Transplant

Date	Event

Notes

Outcome

Uses

Purchased at: _____   Price: _____

Gardening Notes

Plant Name | **Date Planted**

Water Requirements 💧 💧💧 💧💧💧 | Sunlight ☀ ☼ ●

☐ Seed ☐ Transplant

Date	Event

Notes

Outcome

Uses

Purchased at: _____ Price: _____

Gardening Notes

Plant Name | **Date Planted**

Water Requirements 💧 💧💧 💧💧💧   Sunlight ☀ 🌤 ●

☐ Seed   ☐ Transplant

Date	Event

Notes

Outcome

Uses

Purchased at: _____   Price: _____

Gardening Notes

Plant Name	**Date Planted**

Water Requirements 💧 💧💧 💧💧💧   Sunlight ☀ ◐ ●

☐ Seed   ☐ Transplant

Date	Event

Notes

Outcome

Uses

Purchased at: _____   Price: _____

Gardening Notes

Plant Name | **Date Planted**

Water Requirements 💧 💧💧 💧💧💧 | Sunlight ☀ ☼ ●

☐ Seed ☐ Transplant

Date	Event

Notes

Outcome

Uses

Purchased at: _____ Price: _____

Gardening Notes

Plant Name | **Date Planted**

Water Requirements 💧 💧💧 💧💧💧   Sunlight ☀ 🌤 ●

☐ Seed   ☐ Transplant

Date	Event

Notes

Outcome

Uses

Purchased at: _____   Price: _____

Gardening Notes

Plant Name | **Date Planted**

Water Requirements 💧 💧💧 💧💧💧

Sunlight ☀ ☼ ●

☐ Seed   ☐ Transplant

Date	Event

Notes

Outcome

Uses

Purchased at: _____   Price: _____

Gardening Notes

Plant Name | **Date Planted**

Water Requirements 💧   💧💧   💧💧💧   Sunlight ☀ 🌤 ●

☐ Seed   ☐ Transplant

Date	Event

Notes

Outcome

Uses

Purchased at: _____   Price: _____

Gardening Notes

Plant Name	**Date Planted**

Water Requirements 💧 💧💧 💧💧💧   Sunlight ☀ ☼ ●

☐ Seed   ☐ Transplant

Date	Event

Notes

Outcome

Uses

Purchased at: _____   Price: _____

Gardening Notes

Plant Name   **Date Planted**

Water Requirements 💧 💧💧 💧💧💧

Sunlight ☀ ☼ ●

☐ Seed   ☐ Transplant

Date	Event

Notes

Outcome

Uses

Purchased at: _____   Price: _____

Gardening Notes

Plant Name   **Date Planted**

Water Requirements 💧 💧💧 💧💧💧   Sunlight ☀ ☼ ●

☐ Seed   ☐ Transplant

Date	Event

Notes

Outcome

Uses

Purchased at: _____   Price: _____

Gardening Notes

Plant Name | **Date Planted**

Water Requirements 💧 💧💧 💧💧💧   Sunlight ☀ 🌤 ●

☐ Seed   ☐ Transplant

Date	Event

Notes

Outcome

Uses

Purchased at: _____   Price: _____

Gardening Notes

Plant Name | **Date Planted**

Water Requirements 💧 💧💧 💧💧💧

Sunlight ☀ ☼ ●

☐ Seed ☐ Transplant

Date	Event

Notes

Outcome

Uses

Purchased at: _____ Price: _____

Gardening Notes

Plant Name | **Date Planted**

Water Requirements 💧 💧💧 💧💧💧   Sunlight ☀ ☼ ●

☐ Seed   ☐ Transplant

Date	Event

Notes

Outcome

Uses

Purchased at: _____   Price: _____

Gardening Notes

Plant Name   **Date Planted**

Water Requirements   💧   💧💧   💧💧💧   Sunlight ☀ ☼ ●

☐ Seed   ☐ Transplant

Date	Event

Notes

Outcome

Uses

Purchased at: _____   Price: _____

Gardening Notes

Plant Name   **Date Planted**

Water Requirements   💧   💧💧   💧💧💧   Sunlight ☀ ☀ ●

☐ Seed   ☐ Transplant

Date	Event

Notes

Outcome

Uses

Purchased at: _____   Price: _____

Gardening Notes

Plant Name | **Date Planted**

Water Requirements 💧 💧💧 💧💧💧

Sunlight ☀ ☼ ●

☐ Seed   ☐ Transplant

Date	Event

Notes

Outcome

Uses

Purchased at: _____   Price: _____

Gardening Notes

Plant Name | **Date Planted**

Water Requirements 💧 💧💧 💧💧💧

Sunlight ☀ ☼ ●

☐ Seed   ☐ Transplant

Date	Event

Notes

Outcome

Uses

Purchased at: _____   Price: _____

Gardening Notes

Plant Name | **Date Planted**

Water Requirements 💧 💧💧 💧💧💧   Sunlight ☀ ☀(half) ●

☐ Seed   ☐ Transplant

Date	Event

Notes

Outcome

Uses

Purchased at: _____   Price: _____

Gardening Notes

Plant Name | **Date Planted**

Water Requirements 💧 💧💧 💧💧💧

Sunlight ☀ ☼ ●

☐ Seed   ☐ Transplant

Date	Event

Notes

Outcome

Uses

Purchased at: _____   Price: _____

Gardening Notes

Plant Name | **Date Planted**

Water Requirements 💧 💧💧 💧💧💧

Sunlight ☀ ☼ ●

☐ Seed ☐ Transplant

Date	Event

Notes

Outcome

Uses

Purchased at: _____ Price: _____

Gardening Notes

Plant Name   **Date Planted**

Water Requirements   💧   💧💧   💧💧💧   Sunlight ☀ ◐ ●

☐ Seed   ☐ Transplant

Date	Event

Notes

Outcome

Uses

Purchased at: _____   Price: _____

Gardening Notes

Plant Name | **Date Planted**

Water Requirements 💧 💧💧 💧💧💧

Sunlight ☀ ☼ ●

☐ Seed ☐ Transplant

Date	Event

Notes

Outcome

Uses

Purchased at: _____ Price: _____

Gardening Notes

Plant Name   **Date Planted**

Water Requirements   💧   💧💧   💧💧💧   Sunlight   ☀   ☼   ●

☐ Seed   ☐ Transplant

Date	Event

Notes

Outcome

Uses

Purchased at: _____   Price: _____

Gardening Notes

Plant Name	**Date Planted**

Water Requirements 💧 💧💧 💧💧💧   Sunlight ☀ ☼ ●

☐ Seed   ☐ Transplant

Date	Event

Notes

Outcome

Uses

Purchased at: _____   Price: _____

Gardening Notes

Plant Name	**Date Planted**

Water Requirements 💧 💧💧 💧💧💧   Sunlight ☀ ☼ ●

☐ Seed   ☐ Transplant

Date	Event

Notes

Outcome

Uses

Purchased at: _____   Price: _____

Gardening Notes

| **Plant Name** | **Date Planted** |

Water Requirements 💧 💧💧 💧💧💧   Sunlight ☀ ☼ ●

☐ Seed   ☐ Transplant

Date	Event

Notes

Outcome

Uses

Purchased at: _____   Price: _____

Gardening Notes

Plant Name	**Date Planted**

Water Requirements 💧 💧💧 💧💧💧

Sunlight ☀ ☼ ●

☐ Seed   ☐ Transplant

Date	Event

Notes

Outcome

Uses

Purchased at: _____   Price: _____

Gardening Notes

Plant Name | **Date Planted**

Water Requirements 💧 💧💧 💧💧💧

Sunlight ☀ ☼ ●

☐ Seed   ☐ Transplant

Date	Event

Notes

Outcome

Uses

Purchased at: _____   Price: _____

Gardening Notes

Plant Name | **Date Planted**

Water Requirements 💧 💧💧 💧💧💧

Sunlight ☀ ☼ ●

☐ Seed   ☐ Transplant

Date	Event

Notes

Outcome

Uses

Purchased at: _____   Price: _____

Gardening Notes

Plant Name | **Date Planted**

Water Requirements 💧 💧💧 💧💧💧   Sunlight ☀ ◐ ●

☐ Seed   ☐ Transplant

Date	Event

Notes

Outcome

Uses

Purchased at: _____   Price: _____

Gardening Notes

Plant Name | **Date Planted**

Water Requirements 💧 💧💧 💧💧💧

Sunlight ☀ ☼ ●

☐ Seed ☐ Transplant

Date	Event

Notes

Outcome

Uses

Purchased at: _____ Price: _____

Gardening Notes

Plant Name | **Date Planted**

Water Requirements 💧 💧💧 💧💧💧

Sunlight ☀ ☼ ●

☐ Seed ☐ Transplant

Date	Event

Notes

Outcome

Uses

Purchased at: _____ Price: _____

Gardening Notes

Plant Name | **Date Planted**

Water Requirements 💧 💧💧 💧💧💧

Sunlight ☀ ☼ ●

☐ Seed ☐ Transplant

Date	Event

Notes

Outcome

Uses

Purchased at: _____ Price: _____

Gardening Notes

Plant Name   **Date Planted**

Water Requirements   💧   💧💧   💧💧💧   Sunlight ☀ ☼ ●

☐ Seed   ☐ Transplant

Date	Event

Notes

Outcome

Uses

Purchased at: _____   Price: _____

Gardening Notes

Plant Name | **Date Planted**

Water Requirements 💧 💧💧 💧💧💧

Sunlight ☀ ☼ ●

☐ Seed   ☐ Transplant

Date	Event

Notes

Outcome

Uses

Purchased at: _____   Price: _____

Gardening Notes

Plant Name | **Date Planted**

Water Requirements 💧 💧💧 💧💧💧 | Sunlight ☀ ◐ ●

☐ Seed   ☐ Transplant

Date	Event

Notes

Outcome

Uses

Purchased at: _____   Price: _____

Gardening Notes

Plant Name	**Date Planted**

Water Requirements 💧 💧💧 💧💧💧   Sunlight ☀ ☼ ●

☐ Seed ☐ Transplant

Date	Event

Notes

Outcome

Uses

Purchased at: _____   Price: _____

Gardening Notes

Plant Name | **Date Planted**

Water Requirements 💧 💧💧 💧💧💧

Sunlight ☀ ◐ ●

☐ Seed ☐ Transplant

Date	Event

Notes

Outcome

Uses

Purchased at: _____ Price: _____

Gardening Notes

Plant Name | **Date Planted**

Water Requirements 💧 💧💧 💧💧💧

Sunlight ☀️ 🌤 ●

☐ Seed ☐ Transplant

Date	Event

Notes

Outcome

Uses

Purchased at: _____ Price: _____

Gardening Notes

Made in the USA
Columbia, SC
26 November 2024